Seeking a Heart Like His

LESSONS FROM DAVID

BETH MOORE

LifeWay Press®
Nashville, Tennessee

ISBN 9781415869963 • Item 005371620

Dewey Decimal classification: 220.07
Subject heading: BIBLE STUDY \ WOMEN—MINISTRY

Unless otherwise noted, Scripture quotations marked NIV are from
the Holy Bible, New International Version Copyright © 1973, 1978,
1984 by International Bible Society.

To order additional copies of this resource, write to LifeWay
Church Resources Customer Service; One LifeWay Plaza;
Nashville, TN 37234-0113; e-mail orderentry@lifeway.com;
fax (615) 251-5933; call toll free (800) 458-2772; order online at
www.lifeway.com; or visit the LifeWay Christian Store serving you.

Printed in the United States of America

Leadership and Adult Publishing
LifeWay Church Resources
One LifeWay Plaza
Nashville, Tennessee 37234-0175

CONTENTS

INTRODUCTION

What keeps each of us from having a heart like God's?

We can learn many lessons from David. We all have had doubts, fought temptations, battled personal inconsistencies, fallen into sin, suffered losses, and anguished over family problems. David was no exception. He had a multifaceted personality. Our responses to his experiences can be as diverse as he was. He can make us laugh and cry. He can delight and disappoint us. Sometimes we want to be just like him—and nothing like him at others.

David's life and times will cause us to have many responses! He is sure to capture your interest if you let him. And God is sure to change your heart if you let Him. David lived thousands of years ago, yet he dealt with many issues that plague God's people today.

God uses His Word to keep our minds sharp. We never have to worry about getting bored because we never get to the bottom of it: "Open my eyes that I may see wonderful things in your law" (Ps. 119:18). That word for law *(Torah)* means instruction. Even if we don't think of ourselves as loving God's law, many of us have learned to cherish His instruction more than our daily bread!

Psalm 19:1-14 hails God's revelation from its widest context to the most intimate. God reveals His glory to us through nature and His Word to get into our hearts. From the universe to the individual heart, every bit of the revelation is for us.

At the height of David's calling and just before his tumble deep into sin, God spoke the Davidic covenant over David and his family. If we're smart, we'll learn that if such a tumble can happen to David, it can happen to anybody. No one is beyond it, but no one has to go there. David knew before he fell the steps he needed to prevent it. If none of us is exempt from temptation, what can we do to guard ourselves from such pits?

We can know the ordinances of the Lord, but that does not mean we will follow them. The law of the Lord is perfect and His statutes trustworthy (v. 7). The precepts of the Lord are right, and His commands are radiant (v. 8). If we are going to safeguard our lives, we must love the Word, heed the warning (v. 11), seek discernment (v. 12), and live transparently. If we're going to avoid falling headlong into the ditch, we must fear willful sin—whether committed either on purpose or driven by pride.

Meditation is a kind of music that begins in our hearts and ascends to heaven as humming. Imagine that whatever is going on in your heart is you humming a song before God. Is it a song of a critical spirit or hatred? When our minds are set on God, it's a song of praise and great pleasure before Him. When our minds are set on good, pure, and lovely things, our thoughts come before God as a hymn of thanksgiving. We are His playlist.

The Lord knows our every error, every fault, every willful sin, and why we commit them.

All of these thoughts came from the pen of David himself. He knew what to do. Likewise, we know what to do. Most of the time it's not that we lack knowledge. Rather, it's our lack of obedience. God's desire is to reward us. When we do what we know to do according to God, He delights in giving us rewards.

"By them [God's ordinances] is your servant warned; in keeping them there is great reward" (Ps. 19:11).

CHAPTER 1
Humble Beginnings

"The LORD declares to you that the LORD himself will establish a house for you." 2 Samuel 7:11

Have you ever wondered what qualities God may have seen in David's heart when He chose him to be His servant? What does being a man or a woman after God's heart really mean? David's reign began with integrity and administrative adeptness. Let's revel in the best of King David!

After what seemed like an endless struggle, David's dance through Jerusalem as the ark entered the city marked the beginning of a time when life settled down. Second Samuel 7 unfolds as the king in his palace received some well-deserved rest. Verse 1 says, "The king was settled in his palace and the LORD had given him rest from all his enemies."

Sometimes God offers us rest we do not accept. Have you noticed how the body rests more readily than the mind? We may seize the opportunity to put our feet up for a while, but the mind stays in overdrive.

I think David had a little difficulty getting his mind to rest. Certain thoughts occurred to David "after ... the LORD had given him rest" (v. 1). You and I have had similar experiences. Sometimes we are so busy we can't even think. All sorts of plans seem to pour like a waterspout when things get settled.

Ever been horror-struck by your own audacity? This was one of those times for David. Life was calm. Enemies subdued. Perhaps he was sitting on his throne when his eyes were unveiled to the splendor around him. The one who found refuge in a cave was now encased in a palace. He looked around and thought, *What's wrong with this picture?* He responded with shock: "Here I am, living in a palace of cedar, while the ark of God remains in a tent" (v. 2).

Authentic Humility

David and the prophet Nathan shared
concern that David lived in a palace while
the ark of God remained in a tent (v. 2).
Perhaps several virtues can be noted in
David's sudden reaction to his surroundings,
but let's not miss the virtue of humility
so present in his life at this point. He
summoned the prophet Nathan the moment
the thought occurred, as if lightning would
strike if he didn't.

God issued several wonderful and
significant promises through the prophet
Nathan in 2 Samuel 7:9-16. Note that some
were to David personally. Others were to the
nation of Israel as a whole, and several were
to David's "offspring."

*"I have been with you wherever you have gone,
and I have cut off all your enemies from before
you. Now I will make your name great, like the
names of the greatest men of the earth. And I
will provide a place for my people Israel and
will plant them so that they can have a home of*

their own and no longer be disturbed. Wicked people will not oppress them anymore, as they did at the beginning and have done ever since the time I appointed leaders over my people Israel. I will also give you rest from all your enemies.

"The Lord declares to you that the Lord himself will establish a house for you: When your days are over and you rest with your fathers, I will raise up your offspring to succeed you, who will come from your own body, and I will establish his kingdom. He is the one who will build a house for my Name, and I will establish the throne of his kingdom forever. I will be his father, and he will be my son. When he does wrong, I will punish him with the rod of men, with floggings inflicted by men. But my love will never be taken away from him, as I took it away from Saul, whom I removed from before you. Your house and your kingdom will endure forever before me; your throne will be established forever."

These promises capture a wonderful moment between God and His chosen king. We get a fresh glimpse of their highly reciprocal relationship and behold the elements of their everlasting covenant.

The prophet Nathan emerges as a new figure in Israel's history. God sovereignly raised prophets to serve as His voice to Israel. God apparently never intended for civil leaders to have absolute and unquestioned authority. They were to listen to God's voice through His Word and His prophets.

All persons have someone to whom they must ultimately answer—parents and children, employees and employers, kings and kingdoms. God calls prophets to issue His Word, not the messages leaders want to hear.

Wise Accountability

King David sought Nathan's counsel, revealing another important virtue: accountability. David didn't consider himself

above reproach or above the need for advice.
David's statement assumed the question,
"What am I to do about the ark?" His sudden
sense of audacity drew him to accountability.

James 5:16 directs us to an important form
of accountability: "Therefore confess your
sins to each other and pray for each other
so that you may be healed. The prayer of a
righteous man is powerful and effective." Do
you confess your faults and seek counsel
when you feel you have offended God? If so,
do you receive godly counsel?

Sometimes even a fellow believer can offer
wrong advice. We are wise to make sure a
fellow believer's advice agrees with God's
Word. Notice Nathan's initial response to
David: "Whatever you have in mind, go
ahead and do it, for the LORD is with you."
God used David's concern as a teaching tool
for both David and Nathan. He taught them a
lesson on making assumptions.

Perhaps we would be wise to heed as
well. God was teaching an important lesson

through each man. To David God said, "Don't assume that every bright and noble idea in a godly man's mind is of Me." Good ideas and God's ideas are often completely different. To Nathan God said, "Don't assume that a leader I have chosen is always right." The Lord can be "with" a man while a man can make a decision "without" God.

God wanted to dissuade Nathan from thinking David's actions were always right. God was preparing Nathan for a time when he would have to confront and rebuke David. Thankfully, at this point the hearts of both men were right toward God. Their motive was right even if their move was wrong.

God's Gentle Rebukes and Gracious Promises

God's message to His new king began with a gentle rebuke we would be wise to remember every time we have a good and noble idea: "Are you the one to build me a house to dwell in?" In other words, "Have I appointed you to do that?" God reminded David that He was fully capable of appointing a servant for specific tasks. If we are seeking Him through prayer and Bible study, we will not likely miss His appointments. We need to wait on Him even when we have a great plan.

When we wait on God, He gives supernatural strength and accomplishes the inconceivable. Did you notice how God gave David the vision for the temple but his offspring were to build it? God can entrust a vision or an idea to us that may be ours to pray about and prepare for but not participate in directly.

Second Samuel 7:6-7 shows another wonderful principle at work:

> "I have not dwelt in a house from the day I brought the Israelites up out of Egypt to this day. I have been moving from place to place with a tent as my dwelling. Wherever I have moved with all the Israelites, did I ever say to any of their rulers whom I commanded to

*shepherd my people Israel, "Why have you not
built me a house of cedar?"*

To me, God seemed to say, "As long as My
people are on the move, I'm on the move!
You can't tie Me down as long as My people
are mobile!" Isn't He wonderful? The "tent"
to which God was referring was the Old
Testament tabernacle designed by God to
move with the people. That's God's way. You
can't leave home without Him.

John 1:14 says, "The Word became flesh
and made his dwelling among us." The Greek
word for "dwelling" means "to encamp, pitch
a tent … to tabernacle."[1] God was pitching a
tent so He could be where His people were,
so that one day they could be where He was.
Praise His name!

The climactic point in God's message
to David comes in verse 11. Allow me to
paraphrase: "David, you won't build a house
for Me. I'm going to build a house for you."
What overwhelming words. We want to do so

many things for God, and then they suddenly pale in comparison to the realization of all He wants to do for us. Romans 8:32 says, "He who did not spare his own Son, but gave him up for us all—how will he not also, along with him, graciously give us all things?"

David discovered what we often discover: We can't outgive God. God draws His message to a close by issuing what is often called the Davidic Covenant. He issued His promise in the form of a declaration (vv. 11-16). Notice that God's blessings and cursings on David's son might have been conditional (v. 14), but God's kingdom covenant was completely unconditional. The covenant rested on God's faithfulness, not man's.

Interestingly, many years later David reflected on an additional reason why God did not choose for him to build the temple. In 1 Chronicles 28:3 David said: "God said to me, 'You are not to build a house for my Name, because you are a warrior and have shed blood.'" God chose to have His temple built during a reign characterized by peace. I am touched by the mercy of God toward His beloved David. He did not snatch the privilege from him in judgment. Rather, He allowed David's son to receive the honor.

What could be better than being appointed to do a marvelous task for God? For me it would be for my child to do a marvelous task for God. I would happily forfeit participation in the great things of God for my children to inherit the opportunity.

God finally assured David, if I may paraphrase again, "You have the right idea. It's just the wrong time. A house will be built for My name but not now, and not by you. Your son will build My house." If I were David, I would have been unable to contain myself.

We will soon see that David was completely overwhelmed. Our eyes will get to penetrate more deeply into the heart of David as we behold his response to God's gracious promises.

CHAPTER 2

Compulsory Praise

"How great you are, O Sovereign LORD! There is no one like you, and there is no God but you, as we have heard with our own ears." 2 Samuel 7:22

Now I want you to get a chance to respond to similar promises of God over your own priceless life. Ask God to grant you a double portion of His presence and to let you revel in David's response as readily as if you had said the words yourself.

Prone to Worship

We've looked at David's personality from different angles. Few Scriptures allow us to dive into the depth of his passionate soul more deeply than these. We'll taste a morsel of one of David's greatest virtues: While others were prone to wander, he was prone to worship.

Second Samuel 7:18 says, "Then King David went in and sat before the LORD, and he said: 'Who am I, O Sovereign LORD, and what is my family, that you have brought me this far?'"

Have you ever wanted to run and sit before God in response to an answer from Him? Moments like those represent an indescribable intimacy in your relationship with God. When those moments occur, you can't even explain how you feel. Your only response is to go and sit before Him.

When I am overwhelmed by something God has done for me or said to me, I often have to sit a moment and wait for my heart to write words on my lips. Sometimes I weep for a while before I can begin to speak. David might have done the same thing. So intimate were the words God spoke to him through Nathan that he left the messenger's presence and went straight to the One who sent the message.

I have asked the same 2 Samuel 7:18
question more times than I could count, but
not for the reasons you might assume. For
reasons I will never understand, God has
given me opportunities for ministry, and
I praise Him for that. Yet the moments that
most often move me are extremely intimate
and private. Because they are so personal,
I probably will never share in a testimony
some of the most wonderful things God has
done for me. What David was feeling was
not about grand positions—it was about
personal petitions.

We each have countless opportunities to be
overwhelmed by God's goodness. Can you
glance back at your life and say, "Oh, God,
we've come so far!"? Or do you tend to focus
on how far you have to go? Praise Him for
how far you've come and entrust the rest of
your journey to the One who brought you
this far.

After saying, "Who am I … that you have
brought me this far?" David said, "And as

if this were not enough in your sight, O Sovereign LORD, you have also …" (v. 19). How like God to keep giving and giving! David was stunned by God's words of prophecy over his family. What more precious promise could God have given David than to assure him He would remain with his offspring long after David was gone? What peace we can have in knowing God will bless our children.

We can sense a rising tone in verse 22 as if David suddenly broke out in compulsory praises. "How great you are, O Sovereign LORD!" Have you ever experienced David's kind of praise?

At times our praises are planned. For instance, in my quiet time I always plan to have a time of praise and worship. The words and reasons change, but praise and worship are necessities to my daily time with God. At times our praises, though unplanned, are as quiet in our spirits as a whisper—times when we quietly, reverently acknowledge His worthiness. At other times praise is absolutely compulsory—when we would burst if we did not praise; when whispers are hard to contain; when hands are difficult to stay; when knees seem to bend by themselves; when spirit, soul, and body join in compulsory harmony, "How great You are, O Sovereign LORD! There is no one like You!"

Over two thousand years ago a group of disciples were compelled to praise Christ. Some of the Pharisees said, "'Teacher, rebuke your disciples!' Christ responded, 'I tell you,' he replied, 'if they keep quiet, the stones will cry out'" (Luke 19:40).

Now that's compulsory praise. Every now and then we enjoy a moment when we realize with every one of our senses that He stands alone. "No one—no mate, child, preacher, teacher, ruler, or principality—no one is like You." Nothing is quite like suddenly realizing that nothing is like Him.

People Set Apart

David extolled several distinctions about Israel in 2 Samuel 7:23-24:

> *"Who is like your people Israel—the one nation on earth that God went out to redeem as a people for himself, and to make a name for himself, and to perform great and awesome wonders by driving out nations and their gods from before your people, whom you redeemed from Egypt? You have established your people Israel as your very own forever, and you, O LORD, have become their God."*

Israel—I love the sound of the syllables. I love their history. But most of all, I love their peculiarity. Their very identity was in their set-apartness. We often try so hard to blend in. We sometimes resent that God has ordained His people to seem strange to the rest of the world, yet our identity is in our peculiarity.

If David could speak to us from heaven, I am quite certain he would tell us to celebrate our peculiar position in Christ. He would also probably tell us to praise a faithful, covenant-keeping God. I believe when David wanted God to keep His promises in verses 25-26 that he would never have presumed to pray this prayer without first knowing God's will. David concluded with the words, "Now be pleased to bless this house." In other words, "Go ahead and do as You've so generously promised." David believed God and prayed in accordance and anticipation.

Our human nature is self-serving and ambitious. God desires to purify all other motives of ambition in us except the ambition that God would use us to draw attention to Himself and His great name. God's Spirit influences us to transfer personal ambitions to the ambition of His exalted name and character.

Psalm 106:12 says, "Then they believed his promises and sang his praise." Quite possibly David "believed his promises" then "sang his praise." After all, he was accustomed to singing God's praises.

I imagine that David might have ended this intimate time with God in a song of praise. No congregation. No instrument. No hymnal. Just the three-part harmony of his spirit, soul, and body presenting an unscheduled compulsory concert before the ear of God.

I challenge you to do the same. God doesn't care if you have perfect pitch or none at all. Just sing whatever He brings to mind. Any familiar chorus will do. You may feel silly at first, but you will soon be ushered into a precious moment of praise. Tell Him you believe the promises He has made you; then sing. Sing Him a love song.

CHAPTER 3

A Virtuous Man

"David reigned over Israel, doing what was just and
right for all his people." 2 Samuel 8:15

We're studying virtues of the "man after
God's own heart." In chapter 1 we saw
authentic humility. David was filled with
horror that he lived in a palace while the
ark of God dwelled in a tent. We also saw a
sense of accountability as David immediately
sought the prophet Nathan when he feared
he might have offended God. In chapter 2
we saw David's undeniable propensity to
worship. This chapter adds several more
virtues as worthy examples for us to follow.
We return to the battlefield as the nation
of Israel was once again established as a
formidable power. When the dust of war
settles, several important virtues will emerge.

We've seen virtues of David presented as
subtle themes in God's shadow. Now God

directly pinpointed some of David's virtues, allowing him to take a momentary spotlight (2 Sam. 8). I believe God allowed David to be entirely successful at this point in his reign because He could trust David to exalt the name of the Lord. The psalms constantly testify of David's ambitious desire to bring glory to God.

My then four-year-old nephew, Chris, was bickering with his cousins over which video to watch, and Chris didn't get his way. He burst into tears and said, "I don't want to watch that old thing! It's nobody's favorite!" What he really meant was the movie wasn't his favorite. Our entire extended family still quotes him when we don't want to eat at a particular restaurant, play a particular game, or do a particular activity. When I think of 2 Samuel 8, I'm reminded of Chris's statement. The chapter seems to be a dry collection of facts about David's reign. As Chris once said, "This one is nobody's favorite."

Though our hearts may not be drawn to it, 2 Samuel 8 represents the zenith of David's career. God had given him success. David had it all: fame, fortune, power, and position. For just a little while, David handled the unabashed blessings of God with brilliant integrity. Let's seize the moment. We can glean the following virtues from our reading today:

1. A spirit of cooperation

God promised David He would give the nation of Israel rest from her enemies (see 2 Sam. 7:10-11). David did not sit on the throne and simply wait for God to fulfill His promise. He obeyed God's beckoning to the battlefield to participate in the victory.

When God assures us of a promise, He desires that we cooperate in its fulfillment. Other times God directs us to sit still and wait. Wisdom involves learning to know the difference. Whether God tells us to sit, stand, or move, He calls us to respond with a spirit of cooperation. Christ, the coming King, did more to exhibit a spirit of cooperation than anyone who ever lived. Each name listed in the "Hall of Faith" in Hebrews 11 represents a spirit of cooperation. The study of David's life inevitably invites us to ask ourselves some difficult questions. Keep in mind, I never ask you a question I have not asked myself first.

How cooperative is your spirit toward God if 1 is uncooperative and 10 is very cooperative? In your quiet time today, join me in asking God to make each of us keenly aware when we do not offer Him a spirit of cooperation.

2. A ray of hope

David did not annihilate his enemies and simply destroy them. First, God didn't tell him to do so. Second, I believe his God-given motive was to bring the other nations to a place of subservience rather than a place of nonexistence.

The Moabites and Arameans responded similarly to defeat as they both became subject to David and brought tribute (2 Sam. 8:2,6). King David lived in a harsh and cruel time. That he would measure people with a line and kill two-thirds of them naturally offends our modern sensibilities.

We must remember that David lived before the time of Christ. He did not have the advantage of the completed revelation. We cannot judge him by modern standards. What we do see is that David had a concern for the spiritual welfare of the nations. That concern was a giant step forward for a man of his day. David left a remnant among the nations. David exhibited hope for the nations to bend their knees to the King of all kings.

3. A literal dedication to God

At this point David had never confused the source of his strength. He immediately dedicated any rewards to the Lord. If he was praised for his successes, he quickly gave the praise to God. If he was exalted for his successes, he lifted the name of God even higher. When he was surrounded by splendor, he wanted God to have something more splendid. When he returned with gold, silver, and bronze, he dedicated them immediately to the Lord. The Hebrew word for *dedicate* in this passage is *qadhash*, meaning "to hallow, dedicate, consecrate to God, declare as holy, treat as holy; to sanctify, purify, make oneself clean; to be pure."[2]

David immediately dedicated the treasure he received to God. Centuries later, Christ also dedicated the treasure He had received to God. You are the gold and silver—the treasure Christ received because He exhibited a spirit of cooperation and hope when He agreed to die on the cross (John 17:9-11).

4. Justice and righteousness

The definitive verse of 2 Samuel 8 says,
"David reigned over all Israel, doing what
was just and right for all his people" (v. 15).
Consider the two virtues of justice and
righteousness together because God often
treated them as a pair, somewhat like
fraternal twins rather than identical.

According to 2 Samuel 8:15, David did
what was fair (just) and right. Justice and
righteousness bring a specific response in
God's heart: "'Let him who boasts boast about
this: that he understands and knows me,
that I am the LORD, who exercises kindness,
justice and righteousness on earth, for in these
I delight,' declares the LORD" (Jer. 9:24).

Acts 13:22 is a perfect opportunity to
highlight the description God placed on
David, a man after God's own heart. God
delivered a marvelous prophecy about the
Messiah, Jesus Christ, in Jeremiah 33:15:
"In those days and at that time I will make

a righteous Branch sprout from David's line; he will do what is just and right in the land."

Second Samuel 8:15 describes the moment David most clearly and completely fulfilled his calling. For a season the kingdom of David reflected the kingdom of the supreme King of all kings yet to come—Jesus, the Christ, the sovereign Victorious. These were the glory days of David's kingdom. God had given him the keys to the kingdom: justice and righteousness—keys to a kingdom that will never end. Let's consider one last virtue.

5. The wisdom for administration

The wise king knew growth meant a greater need for administration. Chapter 8 concludes with one of the first orders of business: the delegation of authority and responsibility.

Verses 16-18 list the various positions David filled. He had obviously learned an important lesson in his initial leadership of the distressed, indebted, and discontented (1 Sam. 22:2). A leader needs help.

Moses did not learn so easily. Thankfully, his wise father-in-law offered him some life-saving advice when he saw the people gathered around him from morning until night. "What you are doing is not good. You and these people who come to you will only wear yourselves out. The work is too heavy for you; you cannot handle it alone" (Ex. 18:17). A good administrator knows when and how to delegate!

Most of us are in administrative positions in the home, workplace, or church. If you are overloaded right now, decide on some ways you can delegate some responsibilities. Even if we can't see how we are hurting ourselves by taking on excess responsibilities, we need to seriously consider the harm we may be doing to those around us. Jethro specifically said that Moses' unwillingness to let others take some responsibility was not only hurting him but also hurting others. Carrying too much responsibility might hurt not only you but also those you are trying to serve.

Administration was another of David's royal virtues that directly reflects the coming King of kings. As Chief Administrator, Christ will delegate many responsibilities of the kingdom to those who reign with Him (Rev. 5:10; 20:6).

We have focused on David as a man after God's own heart, and we've seen Christ's own heart illustrated. No one was more humble. No one held himself more accountable to God or revealed a greater heart for worship. No one had such a depth of cooperation with God. In all these ways David provided a picture of Jesus. Christ dedicated His every treasure to His Father and will return for us when the Father nods. He will rule in justice and righteousness. As Chief Administrator, He will delegate kingdom responsibilities to the faithful. The characteristics God saw and loved in David are those most like His Son. God has one specific partiality: He loves anything that reminds Him of His only begotten Son. To be more like Christ is to be a man or woman after God's own heart.

Thank you for your dedication to God's Word. May His Word make us more like His Son.

CHAPTER 4

Room in the Palace

"David asked, 'Is there anyone still left of the
house of Saul to whom I can show kindness
for Jonathan's sake?'" 2 Samuel 9:1

Today we continue to study the virtues of
the man God chose to be king. We've caught
glimpses of his humility and desire for
accountability. We've seen him worship with
abandon. We've noted a spirit of cooperation
and felt the breezes of his hope brush against
our faces.

Through David, we catch momentary
glimpses of Christ, not just a man after God's
own heart but also a man with God's own
heart. How wonderfully typical of a proud
and loving father. Through the Old Testament
God raised up men specifically to reveal
wonderful secrets about His beloved Son. As
if He could go only so long without talking

about His Son, the Old Testament is filled with portraits capturing snapshots of Christ.

God sometimes used Old Testament figures such as Isaac, Moses, and David to say, "My Son is like this." David had moments when he resembled God's Son—times when God might have said, "See this guy? His heart reveals what My Son is like." Today we will have the pleasure of seeing a tender aspect of David's heart.

"David asked, 'Is there anyone still left of the house of Saul to whom I can show kindness for Jonathan's sake?'" (2 Sam. 9:1). What emotions do you think David might have been feeling that caused him to ask? David wanted to show God's kindness (v. 3). After Mephibosheth was described as crippled in both feet, David planned to show him kindness for the sake of his father, Jonathan, by having him eat at David's table and by restoring what had belonged to Mephibosheth's grandfather Saul.

Evidently feeling low in the self-esteem department, Mephibosheth bowed down and said, "What is your servant, that you should notice a dead dog like me?" (v. 8). But David did not intend to treat him like a guest. Instead, Mephibosheth ate at David's table like one of the king's sons (v. 11).

Don't you love God's Word? How I praise Him that His Word is not just a book of rules and regulations, of do's and don'ts. The Bible is a book of the heart. Realize God's Word reflects God's ways. His heart must be so tender. Our previous lesson spotlighted the zenith of David's reign. God gave him unparalleled success. David was famous throughout the land, both hailed and feared for being the foremost example of God's power on earth. Now we travel from his public feats to his private feelings.

David knew well the familiar feeling we all know as loneliness. You heard his loneliness as he said, "Is there anyone still left of the house of Saul to whom I can show kindness for Jonathan's sake?" David had conquered kingdoms and subdued enemies. He had servants at his beck and call. All was momentarily quiet and peaceful—and he missed his best friend.

God fulfilled Jonathan's wish and gave David everything, but Jonathan wasn't there to share it. David sought the next best thing. Ziba, a servant of the house of Saul, told him about Jonathan's son Mephibosheth. Ziba's choice of words is interesting. "There is still a son of Jonathan; he is crippled in both feet." His choice of words and timing intimates that he suspected the son's handicap might disqualify him from anything the king sought.

In the encounter between David and Mephibosheth we see several of God's characteristics displayed. Consider with me the following virtues of God.

1. His loving-kindness

Note that David was searching for someone of the house of Saul to whom he could

show God's kindness, not his own (v. 3).
Now consider how God first described
Himself after He proclaimed His name, the
LORD, to Moses: "The LORD, the LORD, the
compassionate and gracious God, slow to
anger, abounding in love and faithfulness"
(Ex. 34:6).

The Lord is first of all kind. Compassionate.
He desires to deal with us first in mercy. If
we refuse to accept His mercy, He often
deals with us in the way He must; but He
is above all kind. As a man after God's own
heart, David was tender. His heart was full of
loving-kindness, and he was anxious to pour
it out on a willing vessel.

2. His initiation of the relationship

"Where is he?" David inquired and
summoned Mephibosheth immediately. Note
Mephibosheth did not seek David. David
sought him. David was the king. What could
he possibly have needed? He had everything.

But he wanted someone to whom he could show God's kindness.

David's action in seeking Mephibosheth pictures God's action in seeking and loving us. God is always the initiator of the relationship, always looking for someone who will receive His loving-kindness!

"The Son of Man came to seek and to save what was lost" (Luke 19:10).

"You did not choose me, but I chose you and appointed you to go and bear fruit— fruit that will last. Then the Father will give you whatever you ask in my name" (John 15:16).

"We love because he first loved us" (1 John 4:19).

3. His complete acceptance

David did not hesitate when Ziba informed him of Mephibosheth's handicap. In the Old Testament people considered physical imperfection shameful, but David summoned Mephibosheth exactly as he was.

How reflective of God's heart! Many wait until they can get their act together before they approach God. If only they could understand, God calls them just the way they are; then He empowers them to get their act together.

Jesus came to minister to the broken and the hurting. Matthew 9:12 tells us about the heart of God: "Jesus said, 'It is not the healthy who need a doctor, but the sick.'"

Picturing the scene when David met Mephibosheth brings me to tears. Imagine the king sitting on the throne, surrounded by splendor. His brightly adorned servants open the door, and before him stands a crippled man. The Word says, "When Mephibosheth son of Jonathan, the son of Saul, came to David, he bowed down to pay him honor." With crippled legs he crept before the king, then he bowed before him. Can you imagine the difficulty for a handicapped man to get down on his knees, press his forehead to the floor, as was the custom, and then rise up? Mephibosheth was obviously humiliated. "What is your servant, that you should notice a dead dog like me?" (v. 8).

Have you ever felt like Mephibosheth? I have. Surely everyone who has ever accepted Christ as Savior has crept before Him, crippled from the fall of sin, overcome by our unworthiness against the backdrop of His Majesty's brilliance. "To the praise of the glory of his grace, wherein he hath made us accepted in the beloved" (Eph. 1:6, KJV)!

4. His calming spirit

As Mephibosheth practically came crawling before the king, David exclaimed, "Mephibosheth!" He knew him by name, just as Christ knows us (John 10:3).

David's next words were, "Don't be afraid." How many times have we seen those words come from the precious lips of our Lord? "It is I. Don't be afraid."

- To the Twelve as He sent them forth, "Don't be afraid" (Matt. 10:31).

- To a bunch of scaredy-cats in a storm, "Don't be afraid" (Matt. 14:27).
- To the three overcome by His glory, "Don't be afraid" (Matt. 17:7).
- To the father of a dying child, "Don't be afraid" (Mark 5:36).

David was very Christlike in this moment.

5. His delight in restoration

David's first desire was to restore Mephibosheth. "I will restore to you all the land that belonged to your grandfather" (v. 7). He had been so hurt by the fall. He had lived with such shame. The king could hardly wait to see Mephibosheth's shame removed and his life restored. David knew about restoration. He penned the words, "He restores my soul" (Ps. 23:3). Perhaps the most grateful response we could ever offer God for our restoration is to help another be restored.

I was nearly overcome when I looked up the name *Mephibosheth* and found that the name means "shame destroyer" or "image breaker."[3] What a precious portrait of our Savior! He has been my shame destroyer and my image breaker!

6. His desire for another son

Mephibosheth came stooped as a servant before the king. The king came to make him a son. He was family—invited to sit at the king's table to partake of his fellowship as one of his own. Imagine the sight when Mephibosheth first limped to the table set with sumptuous delights, surrounded by festive activity, and sat down, resting his crippled legs at the king's table. Hallelujah! We are like Mephibosheth. No matter how many sons the Father has, He still wants more to conform to the image of His first and only begotten, virgin born.

"How great is the love the Father has lavished on us, that we should be called children of God! And that is what we are! The reason the world does not know us is that it did not know him" (1 John 3:1). That's us, all right. One day, when we sit down to the ultimate wedding feast, the lame will be healed, the blind will see, the restored will leap and skip with ecstatic joy! The ministering servants of heaven will surround us! He is a God of loving-kindness just searching for someone with whom to share it. Not just the moment when we first bow before Him and acknowledge that He is king, but every single time we sit at His table. Joint heirs. Sons. Daughters. He is the shame destroyer. The lover of the lame.

I would never have learned to walk with God on healthy feet had I not experienced sitting at His table as a cripple. My emotional and spiritual healing has come from approaching God in my handicapped state and believing I was His daughter and worthy of His love.

I believe God has used His Word to cause

you in some way to relate to Mephibosheth.

Glance over the ways David's actions

picture the virtues of God. Note below

how this lesson has described you.

Isn't God wonderful?

CHAPTER 5
Shunned Sympathy

"David thought, 'I will show kindness to Hanun son
of Nahash, just as his father showed kindness to
me.'" 2 Samuel 10:2

Because Nahash had shown kindness to
David, David wanted to show kindness to his
son Hanun. The Ammonite nobles, however,
led Hanun to believe David had sinister
motives (v. 3) and humiliated David's men
by cutting off their garments and half their
beards. Battle ensued with Joab directing the
Israelites and David eventually joining the
battle (v. 17).

The account of this battle (vv. 1-19)
contains many virtues of David, each further
representing the God who chose him and
placed His Spirit on him. I would like to
highlight three outstanding evidences of
God's character at work in David.

1. An active sympathy for the suffering

David knew better than anyone that a crown did not make a person void of feelings or oblivious to losses. Though Saul was not his father and had often treated him with malice, David had grieved his death. David's throne had been seasoned with bittersweetness because of the tragedy prompting it. Likewise, Hanun was assuming the throne of the Ammonites but at the cost of his father's life.

David believed in showing kindness, especially to those who had shown him kindness. If those who had been kind to David were not alive, he sought their offspring so he could show kindness in return. He attempted such an act toward the incumbent king of Ammon, desiring to express heartfelt sympathy. David had experienced devastation. He had also been in need of sympathy. Psalm 69:20 explains what happened when David looked among men for sympathy: "Scorn has broken my heart and has left me helpless; I looked for sympathy, but there was none, for comforters, but I found none."

Likewise, we may at some time have needed a sympathetic ear or gesture from another person but were unable to find it. Sometimes not finding what we feel we need from others can ultimately bring us benefit. Two direct benefits can result if we are willing.

First, we can become more sympathetic when others are in need. We can become far more sensitive and caring. "Live in harmony with one another, be sympathetic, love as brothers, be compassionate and humble" (1 Pet. 3:8).

Second, we can reach out to a sympathetic God. David exhibited the character of God as he extended sympathy to someone who had experienced loss. You can depend on a sympathetic God in your need. David knew the disappointment of reaching out to others for sympathy and not receiving it, but he learned from his experience that God is always compassionate and sympathetic.

David described the sympathetic heart of God as compassionate (Ps. 103:13), gracious and righteous (116:5), and good (145:9). God is always sympathetic, but His sympathy is not always accepted. David experienced something similar as Hanun rejected his extension of sympathy. The Ammonite nobles attempted to make the new king feel foolish for trusting David's motives. "Do you think David is honoring your father by sending men to you to express sympathy?" (2 Sam. 10:3). A possible paraphrase might be, "Are you some kind of gullible idiot?"

Hanun responded by humiliating David's men. By cutting off their garments and half their beards, he symbolically made them half the men they were. I see an important similarity between David's rejected sympathies, expressed by the humiliation of his delegates, and God's rejected sympathies expressed by humanity's rejection of Christ.

God's most glorious extension of sympathy to a dying world was Christ, His Son. According to Hebrews 4:15, Christ is able to sympathize with our weaknesses because He "has been tempted in every way, just as we are—yet was without sin."

God sent Christ as the delegate of His sympathy to the misery of men somewhat like David sent delegates of sympathy to Hanun. Christ was also met by those who stirred up misunderstanding among the people, just like the Ammonite nobles. Ultimately, His message of sympathy was rejected by the very ones to whom it was first extended, and Christ hung on a cross in complete humiliation. For those who have received Him, Christ remains our sympathizer, ever ready to lead us to a door of escape from temptation or a door of mercy when temptation has turned to participation.

Do you allow God to extend sympathy to you in your pain or loss, or do you tend to reject His efforts? Remember, Christ is the extension of God's sympathy to you. Allow Him to minister to you in your need.

Let's consider two more outstanding evidences of God's character.

2. A fierce protectiveness toward his own

David sent messengers to meet the men to keep them from being publicly humiliated. In effect, he threw a cloak around their exposed bodies and formed a plan to spare their dignity.

I'm not sure we can understand what this humiliation meant to a Hebrew. The thought of being exposed in such a heartless manner would be humiliating to anyone, but to a Hebrew, such humiliation was virtually a fate worse than death. They were a very modest people. Their enemy preyed on one of their worst nightmares. It's different in our present society where many excuse their vulgar participations in pornography by saying, "I simply exercise an appreciation for the human body." Nakedness is something to be shared and enjoyed strictly in the confines of marriage. David fiercely protected the dignity of his men, and God is even more protective of us. In a beautiful soliloquy, God responded to the shame Israel suffered in Ezekiel 16:8-14 by saying:

I spread the corner of my garment over you and covered your nakedness. … I bathed you with water and washed the blood from you and put ointments on you. I clothed you with an embroidered dress and put leather sandals on you. I dressed you in fine linen and covered you with costly garments. I adorned you with jewelry … and I put a … beautiful crown on your head. … You became very beautiful and rose to be a queen. And your fame spread among the nations on account of your beauty, because the splendor I had given you made your beauty perfect.

Ever since Satan exposed shame in the garden of Eden, God's redemptive plan has been to cover it and relieve man of shame's chains. He did so by His own blood. David revealed qualities of his Father, God, when he immediately responded to the shame of his own people with a plan to restore their dignity. He evidenced the protectiveness of God.

3. Vengeance toward the enemies of his people and mockers of his mercy

David did not just formulate a plan to spare the dignity of his men. He took on their enemy himself. God also takes on our enemies when we've been shamed.

Let me assure you, God can take on your enemy with far more power and might than you ever could. When someone persecutes you, your Father takes the oppression very personally, especially when you are ill treated for obeying Him, as David's men were. The battle is the Lord's!

We can see this fact illustrated in several Scriptures, but let's look at just three.

"O Lord, you took up my case;
   you redeemed my life."

LAMENTATIONS 3:58

"Strengthen the feeble hands,
   steady the knees that give way;
say to those with fearful hearts,
   "Be strong, do not fear;
your God will come,
   he will come with vengeance;
with divine retribution
   he will come to save you."

ISAIAH 35:3-4

"But if anyone causes one of these little
   ones who believe in me to sin, it would
   be better for him to have a large millstone
   hung around his neck and to be drowned

in the depths of the sea. "Woe to the world because of the things that cause people to sin! Such things must come, but woe to the man through whom they come!"

MATTHEW 18:6-7

God has extended mercy to every member of the human race. He sent His delegate of sympathy for our sin to hang on a cross as the divine remedy. Those who reject His mercy and mock His motives will be punished sooner or later if they do not repent. Pray for your enemies. Pray they will accept God's delegate of mercy toward them. Pray for a willingness to be a vessel of God's mercy in their lives. A battle is coming and all captives will be kept eternally.

Endnotes

1. Spiros Zodhiates, gen. ed., *The Complete Word Study Dictionary: New-Testament* (Chattanooga, TN: AMG Publishers, 1992), 1295.
2. Warren Baker, gen ed., *The Complete Word Study Dictionary: Old-Testament* (Chattanooga, TN: AMG Publishers, 1992), 2360.
3. Trent C. Butler et al., eds., *Holman Bible Dictionary* (Nashville: Holman Bible Publishers, 1991), 946.

CONCLUSION

Do you see that any one of us could be a man or woman after God's own heart? God is looking for qualities that remind Him of His Son. These qualities are developed in us at no small cost, just as they were in the life of David; but the pleasure of God is profoundly, indescribably worth it!

Let's recap David's virtues. David was humble, accountable, and worshipful. He was cooperative, hopeful, dedicated, and just. He was a righteous king and an effective administrator. He was an initiator of relationships: kind, loving, accepting, restoring, and welcoming. He was sympathetic, protective, and defensive against the wrongs done to his people.

We've seen David at his best, exhibiting the characteristics of the Holy Spirit within him. His heart was patterned after his God's. For a time, he was the greatest king who ever lived—the apple of God's eye.

COMPLETE YOUR

BETH

MOORE

LIBRARY

BETH MOORE's collection of LifeWay Women Bible studies covers relevant topics from believing God to loving difficult people. Each in-depth study helps guide you on your journey to find the answers to life's toughest questions. **How many have you done?**

Go to **lifeway.com/bethmoore** to see the full list and complete your Beth Moore Bible study library.

LIFEWAY.COM/BETHMOORE | 800.458.2772 | LIFEWAY CHRISTIAN STORES

LifeWay | Women

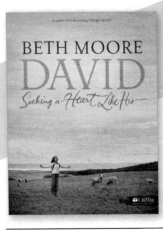